HALSGROVE EVENTS SERIES

THE AINTREE GRAND NATIONAL MEETING

ANDY STANSFIELD

HALSGROVE

First published in Great Britain in 2010

Copyright © Andy Stansfield 2010

British Library Cataloguing-in-Publication Data
A CIP record for this title is available from the British Library

ISBN 978 1 84114 872 4

The Grand National Aintree is a registered trade mark
of Aintree Racecourse Company Ltd

HALSGROVE
Halsgrove House,
Ryelands Industrial Estate,
Bagley Road, Wellington, Somerset TA21 9PZ
Tel: 01823 653777   Fax: 01823 216796
email: sales@halsgrove.com

Part of the Halsgrove group of companies
Information on all Halsgrove titles is available at: www.halsgrove.com

Printed and bound in China by Toppan Leefung Printing Ltd

INTRODUCTION

Aintree has been a race venue for a very long time and, no doubt, will continue to thrill its visitors for many years to come. With this in mind, we wanted to create a book which would also serve to amuse and enthuse its readers during a similar timeframe. In short, we did not want the book to become dated by having a lot of images which related to specific moments, horses or jockeys. What we did want was a book which captures the spirit of the event, across all three days of the race meeting.

The best way to achieve this is not necessarily the most obvious, either. So the reader may sometimes be surprised by images which have been included, and may wonder why others have been omitted. For instance, there are no images of the Grand National runners themselves, due to our licensing agreement with Aintree. Instead, in the images and captions which follow, I have tried to convey some of the atmosphere and excitement of Aintree during a Grand National meeting, largely from a spectator's perspective. The result is a book which, I hope, will be valued equally by both occasional and regular visitors to this three-day meeting, regardless of how much or how little they know about the sport of kings.

The Aintree complex is a large one and cannot be missed if driving along Ormskirk Road heading to or from the motorway network on the north side of Liverpool. It also lies immediately opposite Aintree rail station – probably the single most popular means of arrival, with over 30,000 rail passengers passing through its ticket barrier on the latter two days of the Grand National meeting.

For my own part, although I've photographed many different types of event previously, this was the first time that I've covered an event with the particular characteristics which soon became apparent during the three days I spent there. There are so many focal points besides the races themselves, and Ladies Day in particular proved a fascinating diversion from equine matters. With a prize package worth £35,000 for the best-dressed, there is every incentive for those serious about fashion to make the most of the opportunity to dress to kill. But regardless of the Style competition, almost all the ladies on Ladies Day, the second day of the meeting, turn up at Aintree having made a supreme effort to look sensational. Some, of course, need to make very little effort at all.

Aside from looking good, visitors also need sustenance throughout what can be a long day if they've arrived early to beat the traffic and the crowds using the rail network – and that means more fodder for the photographer too. From bubbly to beer, latté to lager, pies to prawn sandwiches: the choice is almost endless as you browse the concourse, bars and food stands. There are even people down by the track selling cold beer from insulated backpacks, taking away the need to go off to the bar for a refill.

And then there's the noise. As the race card progresses through the afternoon, it is fascinating to track noise levels from the crowd. The low murmur very gradually swells as a race is due to start, hits a sudden minor peak when the horses are off, settles again during the middle part of the race then climbs steadily as the crowd watch the large screens showing the horses approaching the last bend. Once the race is on the final straight the excited babble changes, the crowd's hoarse cries, whoops and curses building to a climax as the finishing line is crossed, then slowly, so slowly falling away to ten minutes or more of sustained feverish banter as wins and losses are debated and celebrated. Throughout each afternoon the clamour, fuelled by adrenalin and a drink or two, gradually increases as winning bets bring ever more confidence and those who are losing get ever more desperate for a win to balance the books. Win or lose, the important thing is, quite simply, to be there.

Andy Stansfield

GRAND NATIONAL COURSE

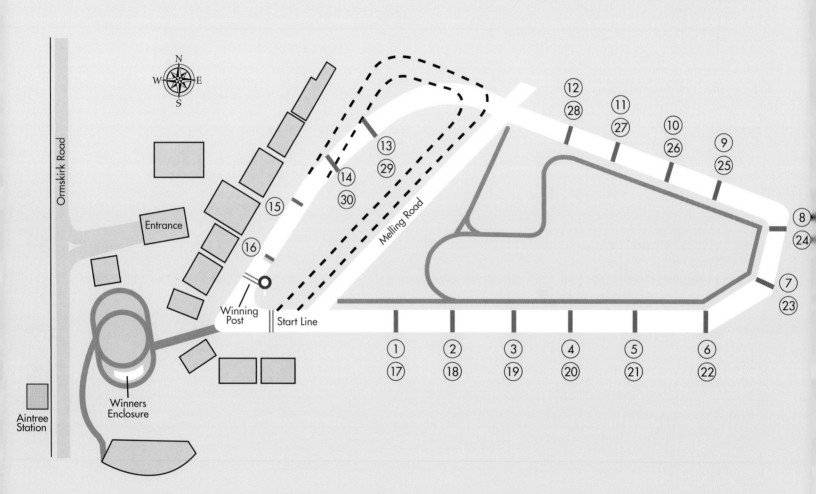

The Water Jump (16)

A 2ft 9in fence followed by 9ft 6ins of water, this fence is situated right in front of the main stands. The Water Jump is the only fence on the Grand National Course to be less than 4ft 6in high. Although visually spectacular, few horses have fallen here and the fence is seen by jockeys as an easy obstacle to negotiate. Nevertheless, four horses fell in 1968 including the previous year's winner Foinavon. In 1955 after heavy rain the fence had to be omitted for the first and only time in race history.

The Chair (15)

The Chair is the highest fence on the National course at 5ft 2in high and 3ft deep, with a 6ft open ditch beforehand. This is one of only two fences to be jumped a single time during the Grand National, the other being the Water Jump. The obstacle was christened after a chair which was placed next to the fence for one of the judges to sit on. Despite its size, this fence sees relatively few fallers, though in 1979 riderless horses causing confusion here meant that nine contenders got no further than The Chair.

Valentine's (9, 25)

Of the two brook-fences Valentine's is not as tricky as Becher's, but still stands 5ft high with an added 6in drop on the far side which demands a nearly perfect jump. It is named after a contender in the very early days of the race, 1840 in fact, who attempted to pull himself up at this fence, only to turn and fall over both fence and brook. Despite this, Valentine went on to finish third.

Becher's Brook (6, 22)

The most famous, or perhaps the most notorious, fence of all is Becher's Brook, named after Captain Martin Becher, the rider who was unseated into the brook in the very first Grand National of 1839. Although not the highest fence at 5ft, Becher's is known for the extra 2ft added to the drop on the landing side, 7ft in all, and is regarded respectfully by even the most experienced jockeys. What's more, it has to be tackled twice.

Foinavon (7, 23)

One of the smaller fences at just 4ft 6in, this became part of Aintree folklore in 1967 when the riderless Popham Down veered across the whole field at this point, bringing down or effectively halting virtually all the remaining runners. However, jockey John Buckingham was sufficiently behind the action to be able to steer his backmarker Foinavon around the chaos and jump the fence. The pair went on to register a now famous 100/1 victory, winning by 15 lengths.

Canal Turn (8, 24)

The ninety degree change of direction after Canal Turn can cause lots of problems, especially with riderless horses. Situated where the racecourse meets the Leeds-Liverpool canal, this obstacle has been the downfall, quite literally, of plenty of riders, notably in 2001 when the riderless Paddy's Return forced eight horses out of the race. Rather than taking the obvious line and cutting the corner, in recent years jockeys have been encouraged to spread out as they approach this 5ft fence.

A racecourse was first set out at Aintree, and a grandstand built, in 1829. When the foundation stone was laid, a bottle of sovereigns was buried in the footings at the same time.

Aintree staged its first Grand National in February 1835. Obstacles then included a section of stone wall and a stretch of ploughed land. During the race Captain Martin Becher was unseated from his horse at the fence which has since been known as Becher's Brook.

During World War I the Grand National was held three years running, in 1916-1918, at Gatwick on the site of the present airport. The race was run over the same distance but with one fence fewer. Although the first race was named the Racecourse Association Steeplechase, for the following two years it was known as the War National.

The first BBC Radio commentary on the Grand National was in 1927. BBC television coverage didn't happen until 1960.

The youngest jockey ever to win the Grand National was 17 year old Bruce Hobbs on Battleship in 1938.

During World War II Aintree served as a base for American troops.

In 1947 the Grand National was moved to a Saturday at the request of the Prime Minister Clement Attlee. Race day was so misty that the eventual winner was accused by some of taking a short cut.

In the mid-fifties Aintree also became the venue for motor-racing. In 1955 Stirling Moss won the British Grand Prix at Aintree, beating the legendary Juan Manuel Fangio.

Although Red Rum is best known for multiple Grand National wins (1973, 1974, 1977) there have been half a dozen other multiple winners including Peter Simple, also the oldest horse ever to win the race (1849, 1853) and The Lamb, one of only two greys ever to win (1868, 1871).

In 1994 the famous comedian Freddie Starr was the Grand National's winning owner, but didn't attend the meeting to watch his horse Miinnehoma come home first because he was superstitious.

In 1997 the 150th Grand National at Aintree was disrupted by a bomb scare and the race ran at teatime on the Monday. This was also the 50th and final Grand National commentary from Peter O'Sullivan, the 'voice of racing' as he was known.

A welcome sight
A roadside welcome to all who approach from Ormskirk Road and Aintree rail station.

Champers anyone?
Room 47, a restaurant a few yards along the road from Ormskirk rail station, offers champagne breakfast on Ladies Day to those travelling by train to the meeting.

Opposite: **Aintree station**
Mid-morning sees throngs of race-goers alight from trains from Liverpool, with the station handling around 30,000 passengers on each of the Friday and Saturday race days.

Charity fundraisers
These ladies collecting for a Down's Syndrome charity sensibly position themselves
outside Aintree station.

Opposite: **Ladies Day arrivals**
These three rail passengers, arriving mid-morning on the Friday, have travelled
down on the train from Ormskirk.

Bitter

These two young ladies brave a bitterly cold wind in sleeveless attire while one of the policemen on hand was actually asking to borrow some gloves from a colleague.

Traffic management
Ormskirk Road is a sea of fluorescent yellow as stewards and police officers, with the aid of traffic cones and hundreds of yards of red and white tape, create a complex system for controlling both the traffic and thousands of pedestrians.

The ride home
At the opposite end of the day, Ormskirk Road is deserted except for a long line of taxis poised to give winners and losers alike a ride home.

Against the flow
Three pedestrians cross Ormskirk Road against a tide of around 700 people who have just alighted from a train.

Elegance
The lady in white, hurriedly captured by the camera as she enters the racecourse on Ladies Day, possesses such a regal presence that she carries space around her.

Security check
Everyone, no matter how distinguished and reputable they look, enters the racecourse through a thorough security check.

What's the plan?

Once through security, friends and family gather together once more to discuss the plan of action. An information board helps first time visitors to get their bearings.

Sense of purpose

Experienced visitors know exactly where they are headed for first, like this gentleman with his purposeful stride into the complex.

Help is at hand

This information stand lies adjacent to the main path towards the stands complex, but staff also move around the whole area and are easily recognisable by their bright yellow jackets.

Customer care
Two of the customer care team pose for a photograph near the parade ring.

Studying form
Visitors arriving early can often be seen studying form somewhere quiet. This gentleman opts for a grassy bank adjacent to the Aintree Mound. This pastime isn't restricted to just the men either *(see opposite)*.

Snapped

Female visitors on Ladies Day, especially those who are distinctively dressed, are easy targets for press photographers who hunt in packs to monitor each entrance for likely subjects.

Snappers
Long lenses are the order of the day on Friday, as Ladies Day visitors become the main subject matter, at least until the first race.

Race technology
Just a few of the dozens of aluminium cases holding technical equipment used to monitor the racing.

Down to earth
Inside the track, this tractor rakes over the sand along the route the horses and their jockeys will take to the start.

Early betting
First thing in the morning there are no queues to put on your bet.

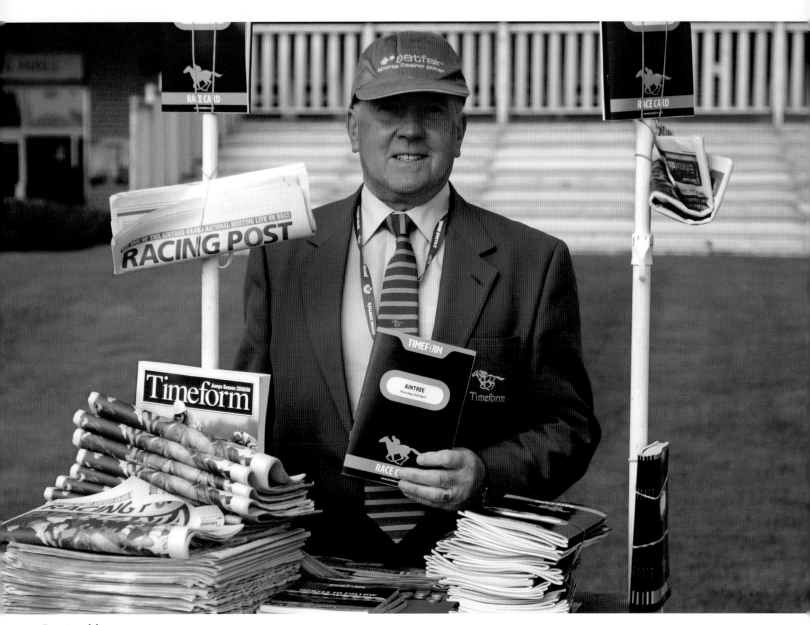

Form guide

If you missed picking up your newspaper on the way to the meeting, there are plenty of opportunities to pick up a *Racing Post* or form guide.

Busman's holiday
This group of off-duty staff from Ladbrokes can't stay away from the racing but they offered no tips. In fact they asked the author for a few.

Up for it
These three gentlemen at trackside are eager to get the racing under way.

Time's getting on
As the clock turns towards the start of the race programme, queues start to form wherever bets can be placed.

Guarding the trophies
The task of looking after the trophies falls to D Squadron of the Duke of Lancaster's Own Yeomanry from nearby Wigan.

Opposite: **Chalk and cheese**
While the soldier attempts to maintain his pose and posture with a suitably detached expression, this lively group of Ladies Day visitors persuade the author to take their photo.

Parade ring
Early in the day the beautifully mown parade ring stands empty but later in the day it will be a sea of colour.

Privileged position
These press photographers take up their positions on the inside of the track ready for the next race. Those sporting a dark photographer's waistcoat take priority over those with beige vests when it comes to access.

Meeting point
Red Rum's life-size bronze statue is one of the best-known locations at which people agree to meet. Before the crowds gather, meeting up with friends or family is an easy business, but once 65,000 other people are sharing the same space it's better to choose a distinctive focal point.

Opposite: **Red Rum**
First sold for just 400 guineas, this world famous racehorse was the only one ever to win the Grand National three times in a career spanning ten years, also coming in second twice for good measure and carrying a total of 24 different jockeys coaxed by five different trainers.

Opposite: **Relaxed atmosphere**
The Red Rum Lawn Bar is still quiet at lunchtime on the first day of the
meeting but it will be packed at this hour on the Friday and Saturday.

Cocktail hour
Kai Joinson from Chester keeps his hand in while it's quiet, one of several bar staff provided by J+Jay Events.

Encouragement

As race participants canter to the start line they pass within feet of Red Rum's grave, a stronger encouragement to win being difficult to imagine.

Mobile barman
One of many purveyors of cold beer with his cooled backpack still weighing heavy on a cold and misty morning, a hot cup of tea being more the order of the day.

46

Horseplay
Both the beer-seller from the previous page and the local constabulary are subjected to the uncertain intentions of this character.

Aintree Mound
This sloping asphalt bank, Aintree's equivalent of Wimbledon's Henman Hill, provides a higher viewpoint for those unwilling or unable to take up places in one of the stands. This young couple are the first of the day to stake their claim to a spot.

Peter O'Sullivan
This bust of the famous racing commentator 'the voice of Aintree for 50 years' was sculpted by Angela Conner and donated by the Duke of Devonshire.

Press tent

A marquee in the centre of the course serves as a base for all the accredited press photographers. Between races up to a hundred photographers can be found here downloading images to their laptops, or working on images already downloaded by wireless file transfer direct from their cameras as they are captured.

Flying solo

This lofty television camera, manipulated by a solitary cameraman, overlooks the winners' enclosure and parade ring.

Rain and cameras don't mix
Down by the track, another TV cameraman is ready for whatever weather is blown in from Morecambe Bay.

From pounds to pints
The old weighing room now serves as Bulmers Original Cider Bar.

Regular visitor
Lisa Elliott, pictured here in the Red Rum Lawn Bar, travels
down from the Lake District for the Grand National meeting
every year.

Hooked and cooked
Lunchtime fare at Aintree is varied, but traditional fish and chips is a firm favourite.

Still a mystery
These three Scots from near Edinburgh tuck into a hearty lunch while the wind whistles around their legs. They declined to answer the age old question about what they wear beneath their kilts.

His and hers
Hats are synonymous with horse racing, especially on Ladies Day, and there are plenty to choose from here.

How about this?
This lady considers how one particular hat will go with her outfit.

Style

Nicky Hambleton-Jones from *Reveal* magazine acts as one of the judges in choosing the most stylish racegoer. The winner is set to receive a prize package worth £35,000 including a brand new Citroen car.

Trading places
Not every cameraman is focused on four-legged performance – this one gets to cover the catwalk instead.

Time to spare
With most visitors arriving a good two hours before the first race, there is plenty of time for a chat with friends or a mooch around the complex.

No comment
One can't help wondering what unvoiced thoughts are going through the minds of each of the elderly couple on the bench in the background.

And baby came too
Children are generally conspicuous by their absence from the meeting, but at least one infant will have something to ask mum and dad about in the years to come.

Parade ring

This is a glorious sight in the spring sunshine, with the blossom out on the trees behind the grassy bank which makes a perfect viewing area. Other visitors prefer to get as close as they can, crowding round the fences surrounding the parade ring *(above)*.

On the box
Television usually covers both the Friday and Saturday races. This cameraman is quite literally on the box, constructed at one end of the grassy bank which affords a good view over the parade ring and its colourful mix of horses, owners, trainers and jockeys *(opposite and overleaf)*.

Fancy a flutter?
It's a while before the racing starts but trackside bookies are already taking money, their raucous cries given as much gusto as that of any market trader.

Opposite: **Two out of three ain't bad**
Mike and Karen are newsagents from nearby Leyland and make a point of attending the meeting every year on the Thursday and Friday, but their business prevents them from coming on the big day itself.

Promises, promises
Money changes hands as thoughts turn to that little note on the right which promises a guaranteed minimum payout of two grand.

Opposite: **The first race beckons**
A suitably refreshing drink now in hand, these ladies start to make their way towards the track itself.

The main stands
The huge overhanging roof of the Earl of Derby Stand juts out prominently on the left with (in order) the Queen Mother Stand, the County Stand and the Princess Royal Stand beyond.

Waiting for the action
Most people form clusters of friends and acquaintances in the sunshine to make the chill breeze off the infield less noticeable.

Almost time for the off

Horses and jockeys alike warm up as they make their way towards the start line on the far side of the course.

Answers on a postcard please
This unusually painted wicket fence stands alone and rather elegantly at that, but its purpose remains a mystery.

Opposite: **Aintree in all its glory**
The fact that you can still see some space next to the track points to the fact that this is one of the earlier races on the card. Later in the afternoon these people will envy the room allocated to tinned sardines.

People watching
Events such as this are fascinating if you enjoy watching people. Body language, gestures and all the little things people do when they think they are not being watched provide hours of entertainment.

81

Sponsors
Just in case you weren't sure who the major sponsor is.

Opposite: **Winning post**
This fraction of a second, as horses and riders thunder past the winning post, is what it's all about.

Feel the buzz

The final moments of a race bring the crowd's collective roar to a climax. But here, in the immediate aftermath of the finish, the noise dies away suddenly to a pronounced buzzing, almost like an electrical charge. This can be maintained for five minutes or more as the crowd discusses the highs and lows of the race and, of course, as the lucky minority collect their winnings.

Race highlights
This horse and jockey make their way back just after the finish as the race highlights are shown on the huge screens around the course.

Twist

The winning jockey of the John Smith's Anniversary 4-Y-O Novices' Hurdle picks up his trophy in the Winners' Enclosure for his ride on the 2/1 favourite Walkon. There is a twist to the tale, too. Ten minutes earlier, the author failed to photograph the finish when his lens was suddenly filled with the blurred face of someone bouncing up and down with joy – it turned out to be the lucky owner, now £130,000 better off, who had been standing beside the unwitting author.

Winners' enclosure
While some collect their betting wins or mourn their losses, others crowd around the winners' enclosure to share the joy of the owner, trainer and jockey.

Mind your heads
This television cameraman manipulates his remote camera above the heads of those around the winners' enclosure and parade ring.

Viewpoints
This friendly couple were happy to be photographed as they stand atop the grassy bank which affords an excellent view over the parade ring. Others adopt a more distant viewpoint on a balcony at the rear of the Earl of Derby Stand *(overleaf)*.

Opposite: **Pick your spot**
The area around the winners' enclosure is always most densely
packed nearest to the track, on the right of this photo.

Fox Hunters
Crowds view the participants in the imminent John Smith's Fox Hunters' Chase on a glorious spring day.

Away from it all
These people watch the race on the big screen on the Ormskirk Road side of the parade ring and winners' enclosure.

Lubrication
Cheering on the horses is thirsty work, needing regular lubrication of the vocal chords.

There's always one
This unusual balloon was spotted in the stands.

Dressed for the weather
These ladies are enjoying the warmth of some mid-afternoon spring sunshine though the day had dawned cold and misty.

Between races
During the interval between events there's plenty of time to chat and compare notes.

Across the track
The County Stand *(left)* and
the Princess Royal Stand
(right) viewed from inside
the track.

In memoriam
Red Rum's grave is situated close to the finishing line opposite the main stands.

102

Soon to be wed
These three friends asked the author to record their Ladies Day outing for posterity as the outer two were soon to be married.

Opposite: **Body language**
The mixture of hand gestures tells a range of stories.

Overseas visitors
This couple made the trip over from Northern Ireland, but Irish accents are far from unusual with Liverpool having a strong Irish community.

Opposite: **Coffee to go**
This beverage stand did thriving trade on Ladies Day, providing all manner of variations.

People watching – again
The author makes no apology for the inclusion of crowd shots as they are a source of great fascination.

Opposite: **Princess Royal Stand**
This is one of three stands providing a huge overhanging roof to protect spectators from the worst of any bad weather.

County Stand

This stand is a complex affair, its roof also being put to good use by TV crews and an array of aerials.

Opposite: **Mending fences**

A crew is always on hand to repair fences after, and even during, each race as and when it's necessary.

Turf repair
Another crew is armed with garden forks, though they don't look quite so enthusiastic about their task.

Another mystery
Why do TV cameramen always leave the protective covers on their cameras even in the best weather?

Up close and personal
Press photographers at The Chair get close to the action. The lady in the red jacket is a liaison officer specifically for the photographers while the fluorescent jackets belong to St John's Ambulance staff.

Photographer fodder
This is exactly the sort of image press photographers look out for on Ladies Day.

Headwear

This member of staff was confined to wearing her uniform on Ladies Day but managed to make up for it by wearing a simple but effective head band. *Opposite*, two ladies tangle feathers as they chat down by the track.

Redhead meets red bow
Deep in conversation by the coffee stand, these two are unaware of the photographer – for now.

Opposite: **Girl talk**
A surprising number of female visitors on Ladies Day arrive in groups.
To the sadness of the male visitors, most go home in groups as well.

Mixed reactions
As a race draws to close, the betting fortunes of these three ladies can be interpreted from their facial expressions.

Ladies Day simplicity (1)
This race-goer, shown here in the midst of an animated phone conversation, has opted for a simple yet stunning combination.

Ladies Day complexity (1)
This group, on the other hand, have between them selected a wide range of hair styles, headwear and dresses.

Ladies Day simplicity (2)
Simple, elegant and
understated is the look here
as this lady perches on a
stool by the parade ring.

Ladies Day complexity (2)
Down by the track, these two spectators
have opted for vibrant colour instead.

Essence of chic
One of the author's favourite images of the whole Grand National meeting, a study of relaxed poise, confidence and style.

127

Mounting excitement
As the day draws on, the stands resound to an exciteable hum fuelled by alcohol or adrenalin or both.

Keeping track
Tracking horses and riders on the far side of this immense course is difficult so the large viewing screens are favoured by most.

Opposite: **Final straight**
From this point on there is only one objective in mind: the winning post.

Thunder
For the press photographer, just a few feet from the nearest horses, the sound of the cheering crowd is drowned by the thunder of hooves.

Opposite: As the riders approach the finish, excitement levels are raised to new heights.

The Mound
Packed to bursting point, spectators on Aintree Mound watch the horses and riders on the final straight while a despondent press photographer holds his head in his hands.

Winding down
Horses and jockeys slow to a gentle canter after the completion of the race.

Oblivious
Elsewhere in the racecourse complex some visitors are oblivious to the excitement as they mingle around the bars and shopping stalls.

Next race
While the crowds in the stands and on Aintree Mound are cheering on one race, participants in the next one are gathering in the parade ring.

Grandstand view
The crowds eagerly wait for the next event on the race card.

Opposite: **Competition**
The horses are still tightly grouped in this race as they head for home.

Winners
Les Mitty and girlfriend Kate Douglas will go home happy after backing a winner, to their obvious delight.

Water Jump
One of the better known fences from the inside of the track.

See and be seen
What better way to finish this collection of images than with a group of local lasses on Ladies Day.
Thanks for the memories.

AINTREE AT A GLANCE

	Grand National meeting attendance			
Year	Thur	Fri	Sat	Total
1984	5,829	6,293	33,961	46,083
1985	10,264	7,861	40,524	58,649
1986	9,962	10,280	51,552	71,794
1987	9,857	11,571	54,141	75,569
1988	12,868	14,573	65,680	93,121
1989	12,239	15,587	74,189	102,015
1990	13,412	17,640	67,235	98,287
1991	13,380	19,012	56,349	88,741
1992	13,330	19,128	55,383	87,859
1993	12,578	19,020	50,492	82,090
1994	13,900	21,303	54,012	89,215
1995	14,188	21,591	88,159	93,938
1996	13,374	24,730	58,203	96,332
1997	14,407	27,450	76,628	114,495
1998	14,984	30,681	46,679	92,344
1999	17,377	30,620	49,400	97,397
2000	18,580	36,420	59,794	114,714
2001	17,910	33,332	52,200	103,442
2002	20,566	42,788	63,511	126,865
2003	22,450	47,430	68,180	138,060
2004	26,200	50,500	70,739	147,439
2005	26,950	53,860	70,850	151,660
2006	26,540	51,940	69,680	148,160
2007	27,060	52,922	68,100	148,082
2008	27,608	53,146	68,360	149,114
2009	25,218	50,722	70,130	146,070

GRAND NATIONAL WINNERS – THE LAST 30 YEARS

Year	Horse	Rider	SP	Going	Field
2009	Mon Mome	Liam Treadwell	100/1	Good	40
2008	Comply Or Die	Timmy Murphy	7/1 JF	Good	40
2007	Silver Birch	Robbie Power	33/1	Good	40
2006	Numbersixvalverde	Niall Madden	11/1	Good-Soft	40
2005	Hedgehunter	Ruby Walsh	7/1 F	Good-Soft	40
2004	Amberleigh House	Graham Lee	16/1	Good	39
2003	Monty's Pass	Barry Geraghty	16/1	Good	40
2002	Bindaree	Jim Culloty	20/1	Good	40
2001	Red Marauder	Richard Guest	33/1	Heavy	40
2000	Papillon	Ruby Walsh	10/1	Good-Firm	40
1999	Bobbyjo	Paul Carberry	10/1	Good	32
1998	Earth Summit	Carl Llewellyn	7/1 F	Heavy	37
1997	Lord Gyllene	Tony Dobbin	14/1	Good	36
1996	Rough Quest	Mick Fitzgerald	7/1 F	Good	27
1995	Royal Athlete	Jason Titley	40/1	Good	35
1994	Miinnehoma	Richard Dunwoody	16/1	Heavy	36
1992	Party Politics	Carl Llewellyn	14/1	Good-Soft	40
1991	Seagram	Nigel Hawke	12/1	Good-Soft	40
1990	Mr Frisk	Marcus Armytage	16/1	Firm	38
1989	Little Polveir	Jimmy Frost	28/1	Heavy	40
1988	Rhyme 'N' Reason	Brendan Powell	10/1	Good-Soft	40
1987	Maori Venture	Steve Knight	28/1	Good	40
1986	West Tip	Richard Dunwoody	15/2	Good-Soft	40
1985	Last Suspect	Hywel Davies	50/1	Good-Soft	40
1984	Hallo Dandy	Neale Doughty	13/1	Good	40
1983	Corbiere	Ben De Haan	13/1	Soft	41
1982	Grittar	Dick Saunders	7/1 F	Good	39
1981	Aldaniti	Bob Champion	10/1	Good	39
1980	Ben Nevis	Charlie Fenwick	40/1	Heavy	30
1979	Rubstic	Maurice Barnes	25/1	Good	34